To

From

Love
Love and beauty

change
Endings
Darkness
Beyond
Each little tiny life

A sad goodbye
A simple wreath
Those we love
A last goodbye

Talking to God
The God of all
The Lord is my shepherd
Our Father
Courage

Hope
Resurrection
A guardian angel
Peace

Thinking of Heaven

Prayers for sad goodbyes

Sophie Piper

Illustrated by Annabel Hudson

LION
CHILDREN'S

Love

Believe in love.
Believe in loveliness.
Believe in heaven.

Love and beauty

I treasure the beauty around me
I treasure the beauty above me.

I treasure the love around me
I treasure the love above me.

When love and beauty surround me
I know for sure God has found me.

change

I will remember the buds of spring
When summertime leaves are green;

I will remember their rippling shade
When colours of autumn are seen;

I will remember the red and the gold
When wintertime branches are bare;

I will give thanks to the God of the trees
Whose love reaches everywhere.

Endings

Day is done,
Gone the sun
From the lake,
From the hills,
From the sky.
Safely rest,
All is well!
God is nigh.

Anonymous

Darkness

The crescent moon
The silver O
That shines upon
the earth below.

The silver O
The waning light
No moon at all
for one dark night.

Beyond

I stand on the sand by the edge of the sea
and watch the waves roll by;
I look to the faraway misty line
where water touches sky.
I look at the shapes of the clouds in the blue
dissolving into space;
I dream of the heaven where God can be found,
where I will see God's face.

Each little tiny life

'Think of the flowers,' said Jesus, 'and how God clothes them in bright petals that last only a day.

'Think of the birds,' said Jesus, 'and how provides them with all they need.

'If God cares this much for the flowers and the birds, how much more does God care about you?'

From the Gospel of Matthew, in the Bible

A prayer for little tiny things
whose little life has flown:
may they be safe in God's great love –
they are God's very own.

A sad goodbye

When little creatures die
And it's time to say goodbye
To a bright-eyed furry friend,
We know that God above
Will remember them with love:
A love that will never end.

A simple wreath

An evergreen
for remembrance;
a faded leaf
for goodbye;
a pure white flower
for trust in God
and hope
of heaven on high.

Those we love

Love is giving, not taking,
mending, not breaking,
trusting, believing,
never deceiving,
patiently bearing
and faithfully sharing
each joy, every sorrow,
today and tomorrow.

Dear God,
You lend us to this world
to love one another.

A last goodbye

Every day
in silence we remember
those whom we loved
to whom we have said a last goodbye.
Every day
in silence we remember.

Where does life come from?
God gives it.
Where does life go to?
God takes it.

Talking to God

Here I am beneath the sky
and all alone in prayer;
but I know God is listening,
for God is everywhere.

May God bless you.
May God take care of you.
May God share your sadness.
May God surround you with love.

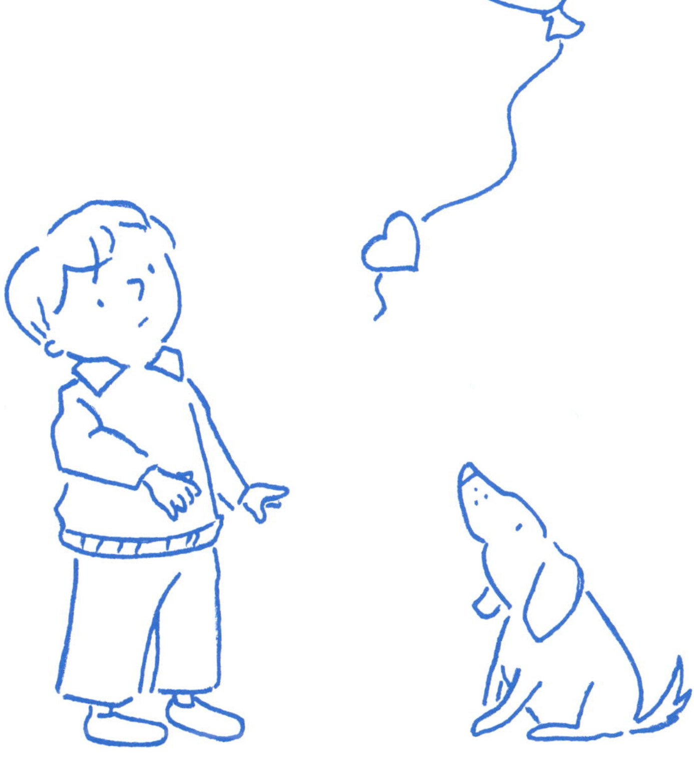

The God of all

God is stronger than all the power in the world:
Even though the wind blows and the trees fall,
Even though the rain falls and the rivers flood;
Even though the earth shakes and the hillsides
   crumble
God's love will never end.

Based on Isaiah chapter 54, in the Bible

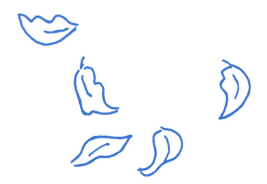

The Lord is my shepherd

The Lord is my shepherd;
I have everything I need.
He lets me rest in fields of green grass
and leads me to quiet pools of fresh water.
He gives me new strength.
He guides me in the right paths,
as he has promised.
Even if I go through the deepest darkness,
I will not be afraid, Lord,
for you are with me.
Your shepherd's rod and staff protect me.

I know that your goodness and love will be with
    me all my life;
and your house will be my home as long as I live.

Psalm 23, in the Bible

our Father

Our Father, who art in heaven,
hallowed be thy name;
thy kingdom come;
thy will be done;
on earth as it is in heaven.
Give us this day our daily bread.
And forgive us our trespasses,
as we forgive those who trespass against us.
And lead us not into temptation;
but deliver us from evil.

courage

The days that lie before us will be hard,
and there is much that will distress us.
But we are determined,
with God's help,
to speak kindly,
to act generously,
and to forgive ourselves and others.

I will not worry,
dear God,
but I will ask you for the things I need
and give thanks.
Give me the peace that comes knowing
that all my worries are safe with you.

Based on Philippians 4, in the Bible

H o p e

Deeply gloomy
Deeply sad
When the day
Goes deeply bad.

Deeply hoping
God above
Will enfold me
In his love.

Resurrection

The autumn leaves were laid to rest
But now the trees are green,
And signs that God brings all to life
Throughout the world are seen.

And Jesus is alive, they say,
And death is not the end.
We rise again in heaven's light
With Jesus as our friend.

A guardian angel

Angel of God, my guardian dear
To whom God's love commits me here,
Ever this day be at my side
To light and guard, to rule and guide.

Traditional

P e a c e

Deep peace of the running waves to you,
Deep peace of the flowing air to you,
Deep peace of the quiet earth to you,
Deep peace of the shining stars to you,
Deep peace of the shades of night to you,
Moon and stars always giving light to you,
Deep peace of Christ, the Son of Peace, to you.

Traditional Gaelic blessing

 *For my Mum*